Trombone

EASY CLASSICS

arranged for brass quintet
by Charles Sayre

easy level

SERIES OF
COLLECTED QUINTETS

TWO CHORALES

TROMBONE

1. O Sacred Head

J. S. Bach
(1685-1750)
arranged by Charles Sayre

Legato tongue throughout unless otherwise slurred.

2. Break Forth, O Beauteous Heavenly Light

TWO FUGUING TUNES

TROMBONE

1. When Jesus Wept

(1746-1800)
arranged by Charles Sayre

*Legato throughout

2. Kittery

VICTORIOUS LOVE
(Amor Vittorioso)

TROMBONE

Giovanni Giacomo Gastoldi
(c1550- c1622)
arranged by Charles Sayre

Play through the piece twice.

IN THE HALL OF THE MOUNTAIN KING 5

TROMBONE

Edvard Grieg
(1843-1907)
arranged by Charles Sayre

AUSTRIAN HYMN

TROMBONE

Franz Joseph Haydn
(1732-1809)
arranged by Charles Sayre

CANON

TROMBONE

Thomas Tallis
(c1505-1585)
arranged by Charles Sayre

C A N A D I A N B R A S S

SERIES OF COLLECTED QUINTETS

EASY CLASSICS

arranged for brass quintet
by Charles Sayre

contents

Welcome to the new *Canadian Brass Series of Collected Quintets*. In our work with students we have for some time been aware of the need for more brass quintet music at easy and intermediate levels of difficulty. We are continually observing a kind of "Renaissance" in brass music, not only in audience responses to our quintet, but to all brass music in general. The brass quintet, as a chamber ensemble, seems to have become as standard a chamber combination as a string quartet. That could not have been said twenty-five years ago. Brass quintets are popping up everywhere — professional quintets, junior and senior high school ensembles, college and university groups, and amateur quintets of adult players.

We have carefully chosen the literature for these collected quintets, and closely supervised the arrangements. Our aim was to retain a Canadian Brass flavor to each arrangement, and create attractive repertory designed so that any brass quintet can play it with satisfying results. We've often remarked to one another that we certainly wish that we'd had quintet arrangements like these when we were students!

Happy playing to you and your quintet.

THE CANADIAN BRASS

U.S. $6.99

ISBN-13: 978-1-4584-0151-9

Distributed By
HAL LEONARD

50488763   9 781458 401519

0 73999 88763 1

HL50488763

HAL•LEONARD®
CORPORATION
7777 W. BLUEMOUND RD. P.O. BOX 13819 MILWAUKEE, WI 53213